SERIES 235

In this book, we will learn what climate is,
how and why it is changing and what that
means for life on Earth.

LADYBIRD BOOKS

UK | USA | Canada | Ireland | Australia
India | New Zealand | South Africa

Ladybird Books is part of the Penguin Random House group of companies
whose addresses can be found at global.penguinrandomhouse.com.

www.penguin.co.uk www.puffin.co.uk www.ladybird.co.uk

Penguin
Random House
UK

First published 2023
001
Copyright © Ladybird Books Ltd, 2023
Printed in Italy

The authorized representative in the EEA is Penguin Random House Ireland,
Morrison Chambers, 32 Nassau Street, Dublin D02 YH68

A CIP catalogue record for this book is available from the British Library
ISBN: 978–0–241–54566–9
All correspondence to:
Ladybird Books
Penguin Random House Children's
One Embassy Gardens, 8 Viaduct Gardens
London SW11 7BW

MIX
Paper from
responsible sources
FSC® C018179

Climate Change

A Ladybird Book

Written by HRH The Prince Charles,
former Prince of Wales,
Tony Juniper and Emily Shuckburgh

Illustrations by Aleesha Nandhra

What is climate?

While weather can change from day to day, "climate" is the term used to describe the typical weather for a particular area. For example, a place's climate may be hot and dry or cold and wet. Climate information is collected over a long period of time, usually a couple of decades. On Earth, the atmosphere, the oceans, the land, ice, people, plants and animals, and a light and heat from the Sun are connected. This determines climate.

The Earth's atmosphere is a thin layer of gas above the Earth. Most of the atmosphere is nitrogen (N_2) and oxygen (O_2), but there are other gases in the atmosphere, too. Some of these gases are called "greenhouse gases" because, like the glass in a greenhouse, they keep the Earth warm. They do this by stopping some of the Sun's heat from leaving the Earth. They help to keep Earth at a temperature where life thrives. Without greenhouse gases, the Earth would be very cold, but if we have too many greenhouse gases, the Earth gets very hot. Carbon dioxide (CO_2) is a very important example of a greenhouse gas.

Scientists study the Earth's atmosphere from satellites and from the ground, and their studies show that the amount of greenhouse gases in the atmosphere is growing. This is making the temperature on Earth get warmer, and this warming is having a big effect on the climate and the daily lives of all the people in the world.

A history of climate change

Over millions of years, the climate on Earth has changed many times. It has been very, very cold, with lots of snow and ice everywhere. It has also been very, very hot, with forests of trees growing in the Arctic and Antarctica.

For the past 2.6 million years, the Earth's climate has changed in a cycle – sometimes warmer and sometimes colder. This cycle comes from the natural changes in the way the Earth moves round the Sun. The climate also varies with changes in the strength of heat coming from the Sun, and the effect of volcanoes and dramatic weather patterns.

There have been many "ice ages" in the Earth's past. At these times, there was a huge area of thick ice over North America, Europe and Asia. Frozen water on land meant there was less water in the ocean, and sea levels across the Earth were about 120 metres (394 ft) lower than they are today. There were also fewer people in the world then – scientists believe only about 130,000 people lived in Europe. Between the ice ages, the Earth was warmer, the sea levels were higher, and there were different plants and animals living on the Earth.

While these past changes in the Earth's climate were caused by natural factors, the climate changes being seen now are not natural. They are happening as a result of the actions of people, and they are happening at a very fast rate.

Heating up

For decades, scientists have talked about climate change and the warming of the Earth. Information and data collected from the last 150 years shows that the average temperature of our planet has gone up. The information we get from weather stations, ships and buoys shows that, over the first two decades of the twenty-first century (2001–2020), the Earth's temperature was almost 1°C (1.8°F) hotter than 1850–1900. In 2021, it was 1.1°C (2.0°F) hotter. This is a big increase, and scientists are worried about it.

Each of the past four decades has been warmer than the one before, and we are seeing the effects of this all over the world. Weather patterns are changing, the ocean is getting warmer, snow and ice are melting, and sea levels are rising.

The effects of a hotter planet can cause many problems for the people on Earth, and for the beautiful plants and animals that live here, too. It could mean that there is not enough food and water for everyone; it could have a damaging effect on people's health; and it could mean that some people are either forced to move from where they live or have a poorer quality of life.

We need to act now to stop climate change and to make a better future for our world. If we do not act now, we will put the future of our world in danger.

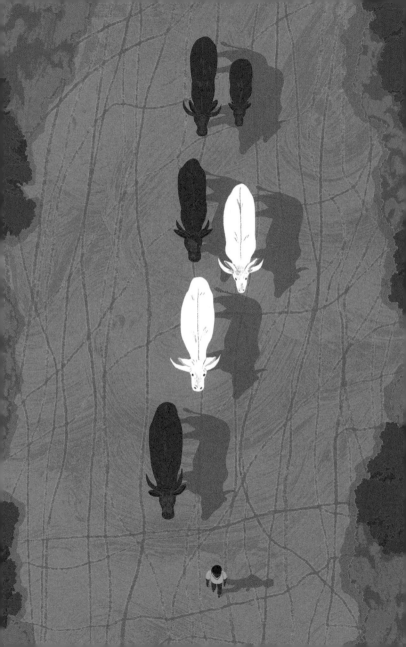

Climate change today

Across the world, there are many thousands of scientists who study the climate and climate change. Their work reveals that people are the main cause of climate change today. Many of the things that people do increase the amount of greenhouse gases – carbon dioxide, methane (CH_4), nitrous oxide (N_2O) and others – in the atmosphere. This makes the Earth hotter.

Plants and animals are made from carbon (C). When they die, some of their remains get buried and form deposits in the ground. Over millions of years, these remains of living things can transform and turn into fossil fuels like coal, oil and natural gas. People then burn these fossil fuels in their homes, in factories, and in cars, buses and planes. When we burn fossil fuels, the carbon that was trapped inside them millions of years ago is released back into the atmosphere as carbon dioxide.

Plants take in carbon dioxide from the atmosphere. When trees in forests are cut down (a process known as "deforestation"), there are fewer plants available and the amount of carbon dioxide in the atmosphere increases.

Modern farming techniques can actually produce methane and nitrous oxide, releasing them into the atmosphere. Greenhouse gases are also created when things are produced in factories and when things we throw away start to rot.

Carbon and climate

Carbon dioxide is a very important gas for life on Earth. Plants need it to live. They take in carbon dioxide, use the carbon to grow and then put oxygen back into the atmosphere. People and animals then take in this oxygen, as well as the carbon from plants, use it to live, and put carbon dioxide back into the atmosphere. When plants and animals die, the carbon in them can go back into the atmosphere as carbon dioxide, or it can go into the ground in their remains.

In this way, the carbon on Earth moves between the land and the atmosphere, and between the oceans and the atmosphere, too. This movement is called the "carbon cycle".

Our oceans, land and forests naturally absorb and store about half the carbon dioxide that people put into the atmosphere. The other half stays in the atmosphere. It can't escape to space because there is no way for it to get out.

Every year, people put about 40 billion tonnes of carbon dioxide into the Earth's atmosphere. Most of this comes from burning fossil fuels and from manufacturing in factories, but some of it comes from deforestation and from changing the way we use the land.

As a result, the Earth has now warmed by over 1.1°C (2°F), and this is causing problems for all life on Earth. We need to stop putting carbon dioxide into the atmosphere and keep the temperature increase to no more than 1.5°C (2.7°F).

Measuring carbon dioxide

The carbon dioxide levels in the atmosphere today are much higher than at any time in the last 800,000 years. We know this because of the work of scientists who study very deep and old ice in Antarctica.

The ice in Antarctica has formed over hundreds of thousands of years. Over this time, snow fell and made layers that built up to make the thick ice that we see in Antarctica today. Every time the snow fell, small amounts of air also got trapped inside the ice and could not get out. Scientists can take ice cores from more than 3,000 metres (9,840 ft) down to find air from hundreds of thousands of years ago. By studying this air, they can find out about the atmosphere in the past. These ice cores show that the changes in the last century are not part of Earth's natural cycles.

Studies of ice cores and ocean sediment show that carbon dioxide is going into the atmosphere more quickly now than at any time in the past 50 million years. Today's changes in carbon dioxide levels are not because of natural causes but because of people.

Most of the carbon dioxide in the atmosphere today will stay there for decades, centuries or thousands of years. This means that we will see the effects of this carbon dioxide for a long time to come, and the more we release, the bigger the effects will be.

The energy we use

Energy is everywhere. "Energy" is the word scientists use to describe the ability to do work or provide movement. Energy powers our world. We use it to drive cars, make products, run computers, light offices and heat homes.

Energy can be converted from one form to another. For example, food contains chemical energy that the body can store for later or use to create movement. The chemical energy in coal or wood can be extracted to create light, heat or electrical energy.

As human civilization continues to develop, we require more and more energy to power our lives and function in different societies round the world.

Humans have built factories, developed cars and planes for travel and invented new technologies. Today, people use 20 times more energy than they did in 1850 and, as the number of people in the world grows, the amount of energy we need also grows.

Today, fossil fuels, such as coal, oil and natural gas, are used most often to provide this energy. But burning fossil fuels releases carbon dioxide into the atmosphere, and this is the main contributor to climate change. To stop climate change, people need to stop using fossil fuels for energy.

Fossil fuels

Over time, the types of energy humans use have changed. In the past, we burned wood and used energy from the wind and from the water in rivers. Today, more than 75 per cent of the energy we use comes from fossil fuels.

Fossil fuels are being taken from the ground to burn for energy at a rapid rate. Unlike wind, water or the Sun, they are considered a "non-renewable" energy source. This means once they are used they cannot be used again.

These carbon-based materials (coal, natural gas, petroleum and crude oil) are used to power our modern world. When we burn fossil fuels, the carbon inside them is put into the atmosphere as carbon dioxide.

The amount of carbon dioxide we can put into the atmosphere before we reach the risk of dangerous levels of warming is called a "carbon budget". The more carbon budget we use now, the less we have to use in the future.

For the Earth's warming to stay below 1.5°C (2.7°F), the carbon budget is less than 2,900 billion tonnes. But scientists think that, from 1850 to 2019, we put around 2,400 billion tonnes of carbon dioxide into the atmosphere. This means we have less than 500 billion tonnes left. Countries must now work together to plan how to use the remaining carbon budget carefully.

Deforestation

Across the world, forests take in carbon dioxide and hold it in their trees, plants and the soil under them. When we cut down trees, in an act called "deforestation", most of that carbon dioxide goes back into the atmosphere.

Deforestation puts a lot of carbon dioxide into the atmosphere and also destroys the habitats of animals, some of which are now extinct. Tarpans (a species of wild horse) and aurochs (a species of wild cow) disappeared when they were hunted and the forests where they lived were cleared across Europe, Asia and North Africa.

In the last century, the deforestation of rainforests in some parts of the world has become a big problem. Some of these rainforests are on soils that hold a huge amount of carbon, including soils called "peat". These soils have taken in carbon slowly over thousands of years.

When people destroy these rainforests, they not only remove the trees but also damage the soil under the trees, and this puts carbon dioxide back into the atmosphere. Farming can also damage soils and put even more carbon dioxide into the atmosphere.

Today, people are still cutting down forests, often to build farms, mines, roads or cities. Over the last 150 years, 25 per cent of the carbon dioxide put into the atmosphere by people has been because of deforestation.

The effect on weather

Heatwaves, droughts, floods and storms are all examples of what is known as "extreme weather". A heatwave is very hot weather for many days, and a drought is very little rain for a long time. There has always been extreme weather on Earth, but recent studies show that climate change has increased the risk of extreme weather. Many places are having their highest-ever temperatures, and other places are having more rain than ever before.

In summer 2022, England had record temperatures exceeding 40°C (104°F), and in 2020, there was an extreme heatwave in Canada, with the temperature reaching nearly 50°C (122°F). Over recent years, huge forest fires in Australia, Russia, Brazil and the USA have followed droughts and high temperatures, causing more carbon dioxide to be released. In Europe in 2003, there was a summer heatwave that killed tens of thousands of people.

Huge storms have hit countries around the world, with high winds and flooding damaging property, costing billions of pounds worth of damage and causing many people to die.

The effects of extreme weather are not only dangerous for people but also affect many other living things that share our world. The number of heatwaves, droughts, floods and storms we are seeing is increasing in many places. Extreme weather is now becoming normal for many people.

The effect on ice and sea levels

The warming of the Earth is causing the Arctic sea ice to melt. At the end of the summer melting season, the Arctic sea ice is now typically one third smaller than it was at the end of the twentieth century. In other words, the size of the ice lost is larger than the UK, Ireland, France, Spain, Germany, Italy, Portugal, Belgium and the Netherlands put together.

Studies show that sea levels across the world are increasing. As the Earth gets warmer, the water in the ocean gets warmer, too. This heat makes the water expand – get larger and take up more room – increasing sea levels. Heat also causes the land ice in Greenland and Antarctica to melt, again causing sea levels to rise.

When sea levels increase, floods from storms can be more dangerous, especially for people living near the sea or other waterways. Many of the world's biggest cities, like Shanghai in China, Jakarta in Indonesia and Mumbai in India, are very close to the sea. Higher sea levels put these cities in danger of flooding and the people who live there at risk.

The floods in New York City in the USA in 2012 showed the damage that big storms can do. These floods damaged homes and other buildings, and cut the electricity supply. This meant people had no heat, no light and no way to cook food or heat water. The damage caused by big storms can have an effect for years and can cost billions of pounds.

The effect on animals

Climate change is causing problems for many of the animals that live on Earth. Changes in temperature, the seasons (spring, summer, autumn and winter) and the amount of food and water animals can find all make life much more difficult for animals in different parts of the world.

When changes to the climate are slow, animals can find ways to adapt and live with the changes. But the climate change happening now is happening very quickly, and it is damaging for many of the living things on Earth. At the same time, people are taking more land to develop and build towns and cities and to grow food in fields. All of these things take habitats away from animals.

Together, climate change and habitat loss are making life very difficult for all kinds of wildlife, and some animals are at risk of becoming extinct. For example, as a result of Arctic ice melting, polar bears are finding it very difficult to hunt for food and to survive. Many Australian animals are also at risk due to habitat loss – the yellow-footed rock wallaby, the golden-shouldered parrot and the Lumholtz's tree-kangaroo are among those at risk of disappearing completely.

In the future, we may not have the large numbers of different animals and plants that we see on Earth today due to the damage caused by climate change. This would make the world a poorer, sadder, less diverse and less colourful place.

1. Lumholtz's tree-kangaroo
2. Yellow-footed rock wallaby
3. Golden-shouldered parrot

The effect on human health

Climate change can affect our ability to grow food and our access to fresh water. It can increase the spread of disease, and high temperatures can cause illness. As a result, climate change can affect our physical and mental health.

Much of the food we buy at supermarkets starts its life in a field or on a farm. But crops need the right conditions to grow properly. Droughts and floods have a very damaging effect on how much food we can grow.

When plants struggle to grow, this can increase the price of food, which means poorer people are unable to buy it, forcing some people to go hungry. Some plants will grow better in a different climate, but scientists think that the effects of climate change will make it harder to grow enough food for everyone in the future.

Across South Asia and China, water for drinking and farming comes from large rivers. The water in these rivers comes from rain, snow and ice melting in the Himalayan mountains. Climate change can have an effect on all of these things. This might mean less fresh water in the rivers and less water for people to drink and use.

When people do not have the food and water they need, it can cause problems in our communities. Sometimes, people move from their homes to try to find a better place to live or to find enough food and water.

The world's problem to solve

Climate change is a problem for the world. One country on its own cannot find the solution – all countries need to work together on this problem, developing ideas for change in a way that is good for the Earth and not damaging to it. Only by working together can we build a positive future for all.

People all over the world have asked countries to do more to stop climate change. In 2015, in Paris, France, nearly 200 countries came together to agree to find ways to cut the amount of greenhouse gases they put into the atmosphere, to protect forests and to increase the health of their soils. But the steps they agreed to take were not enough.

In 2021, in Glasgow, Scotland, these countries came together once more. They agreed to do more to cut greenhouse gas emissions, to protect nature and to do more in the future, but the promises were still not enough to stop the Earth heading towards a dangerous level of warming.

To stop the Earth's warming going above 1.5°C (2.7°F), people need to cut greenhouse gas emissions immediately and stop putting any carbon dioxide into the atmosphere by 2050. This will help to stop further climate change, but people will still have to live with the effects of the climate change we are already experiencing. So, in Glasgow, the countries also had to agree to help protect people from existing dangers, such as extreme weather and rising sea levels.

Positive steps

Companies across the world are now looking at new ways of making the things we need, to ensure we have enough food, water and goods, while reducing climate-changing pollution. They are inventing new technologies and creating new jobs to help find solutions to climate change that could make life better in many different ways.

Cleaner sources of energy are being developed and adopted by companies. All the large car companies are now making cars that use electricity, and new types of fuels are being developed for aeroplanes, including fuels produced from plants or waste.

Building companies are making new houses that are comfortable, use very little energy and are cheaper to live in.

In some forests, people will cut down a tree and then plant a new one in its place. This is called "zero deforestation". A lot of companies are now making the idea of zero deforestation part of everything they do.

Farmers are finding ways of producing food that help to increase carbon levels in soil. They might do this by changing the plants that they grow or by not always growing the same crops. They might sometimes grow plants on the land then keep animals on it. These steps can help to make soils healthy, and good soils also hold more water. This means that they can protect plants from drought.

Cleaner energy sources

To make a better future for the Earth, we need to cut the amount of greenhouse gases being released into the atmosphere. We need to stop burning fossil fuels and to only use cleaner sources of energy in the future.

We can get clean energy from a number of places – the wind, the Sun, plants, the water moving in rivers and the ocean, hot rocks under the ground and other new ways of making energy. Energy generated from the Sun and wind made up just 7 per cent of the energy we used in 2021, but this is growing quickly. This type of energy is called "clean" because it is much better for the Earth than fossil fuels, as it does not put any greenhouse gases into the atmosphere when it is generated. Nuclear energy also puts very few greenhouse gases into the atmosphere, but it is expensive.

Countries can speed up change by making it cheaper to make and use clean energy, and more expensive to make and use fossil fuels. Asking companies to develop clean ways of doing things can create jobs, stronger communities and a better climate for everyone.

We must also try not to use more energy than we need. We need to find ways to use less energy in our homes and in factories. People are now using computer systems in their homes to monitor the amount of energy they use, as well as converting to cleaner energy sources in the home.

Campaigning for change

People have been slow to make the changes needed to stop pollution causing climate change. Across the world, people expect to have cheap food and energy, and this is especially important for poor and disadvantaged people. Many food and energy companies also make a lot of money doing things the way they always have, by clearing forests and mining fossil fuels, so they are not very motivated to change.

Change can be unsettling and it can also cause prices to temporarily increase as new technology is developed. Global leaders, such as prime ministers and presidents, might avoid putting new laws to cut pollution in place to avoid upsetting big companies as well as the general public. This means things do not change as quickly as they need to. This is also why it is so important for everyone who knows about climate change to ask for more to be done.

Young people have been very vocal in saying that more must be done. They have told governments and companies to make changes before climate change causes too much damage. Some children have organized school strikes to promote action on climate change. They have also taken action themselves, by saving energy and planting trees.

The more that people know about climate change and ask for something to be done, then the more likely it will be that countries and companies will do what is needed.

Reduce, reuse, recycle

The Earth and its living things run in cycles. The water cycle and the carbon cycle are very important patterns for life on Earth. Soils use the good things from dead plants to grow new plants. In natural cycles, everything is used again.

But, in today's world, people often do not do things in cycles. We make things, and then we use them. When we finish using things, we throw them away. When we throw things away, they often go into the land, the atmosphere or the oceans. We do not use them again, or get back the energy or the resources we used to make them.

This means that we use a lot of energy and natural resources. But doing things in cycles does not use as much energy or natural resources, and it does not put so much carbon dioxide into the atmosphere. Companies need to do things in new and different ways. They must try to find ways of using everything again and throwing nothing away – just like natural cycles.

We need to look at the natural cycles on Earth and try to do things in the same way. Many companies are already using these ideas to make new things and to help stop climate change. For example, companies are using natural cycles to develop new fuels.

Reduce

Reuse

Recycle

One Earth

For hundreds of years, we have used more and more from the natural world, but there is still only one Earth.

The number of people living on Earth grows every day, and every day we have a bigger and bigger effect on the Earth. For the communities of the world to have a positive future, we must find ways of living on the Earth without damaging it in the way we do today.

We are already seeing the bad effects of climate change, but things may be much worse in the years ahead. We need to see that the Earth is in danger, and we must act now to find solutions before it is too late.

Everyone must work towards stopping climate change and protecting and restoring nature. On our own and together, young and old, we can all help. Every day we can decide to do things that cut the amount of carbon dioxide we put into the atmosphere. Every day we can take positive steps to keep the natural world healthy. We have had a bad effect on the natural world for too long, and we need to stop now and instead work towards a better future.

Only when we are good to the Earth, by protecting and preserving it, can the Earth be good to us.

I do hope you found this little book about climate change interesting and that it has made you want to help do something. It is a truly huge challenge, but the good news is that everyone can make a difference – particularly when we decide what we buy and how we do things every day.

Ever since I was a young teenager I have been deeply worried about the way we have shaped our world. For a long time we have produced our food and created the things that make our lives easier without seeing that this has broken Nature's ability to keep every form of life healthy. Producing so much pollution, destroying so many forests by cutting down millions of trees, polluting the sea with vast amounts of tiny pieces of plastic or putting chemicals on the land to speed up the way plants grow has all caused so many birds, animals, fish and insects to disappear. All these forms of life are known as 'biodiversity' and its loss will impact life disastrously not just on the land, but in the oceans where vast amounts of plastic now floats in tiny pieces in seas around the world.

These are just a few of the many serious problems we have caused, all of them made worse by global warming and climate change which, as this book has shown, are already affecting the planet's ability to keep everything stable and all of us healthy.

It may seem worrying, but over the years I have also discovered there are lots of solutions to these problems, which point to how we can do things better.

The first thing we can all do is very simple. We can understand how Nature works – how every flower and insect, all the tiny bacteria and creatures in the soil, every bird, animal and human needs everything else. Once we see that all forms of life are connected, we realise that we are part of a world wide web and that if we break the links that hold the web together the whole web starts to fall apart.

In the past we did not understand this. My great, great, great Grandmother was Queen Victoria and in the Victorian Age there was a revolution in how the world worked. Great cities were built and vast quantities of coal were burned to power factories, ships and trains. No one knew that this would help cause climate change, but today we do and we have begun to find cleaner ways of doing all those things. There are lots of new technologies that are helping to solve a wide range of problems. We also know that if we plant and grow new forests consisting of a wide range of different species, those trees will breathe in the carbon dioxide that is causing the climate to change – and those trees offer all sorts of other benefits too.

They offer a home to many kinds of wildlife. The trees soak up water so they can help reduce flooding. Not only do they help ensure rainfall around the world and produce vital oxygen for us all to breathe, but they also make the soil more fertile which allows other vegetation to grow, and they provide food for all kinds of important insects like bees that pollinate the plants that we grow to make our food. This all happens because Nature works in a very efficient way. It produces so much without creating any waste. Everything is reused over and over again. This is a lesson we need to learn and an example we need to follow as part of a circular bio-economy.

When you understand how important trees are and how nothing goes to waste, you start to see just how completely all life on Earth is inter-connected. I think this is a wonderful thing. It is so special that I call it 'sacred.' If something is sacred to us, it means it is so important that we have a duty to look after it. That is why we have a duty to manage Nature in a careful way to help it be healthy, rather than making it ill. This means that if we profit from Nature by enjoying good food or even by playing a computer game, we have to make sure that Nature profits too. It is a simple relationship. If we look after Nature, then we also look after ourselves.

I am pleased to see that children across the world understand this and are now raising the alarm and calling for big changes to happen. Their efforts have emphasised the importance of caring about what life will be like in the future – there is a lesson in this for us all.

Even compared with a few years ago, many more people are now much more aware of the need for change. There are also new laws and big, worldwide agreements in place which, if we follow what they say, will lead us to finding the solutions we need. For example, some of the biggest companies in the world